EFFECTIVE RETAIL MANAGEMENT

(a booklet of hints and tips for retail businesses)

"I'm from down the street. A customer
ordered our wine because it's better than yours.

By Nigel Toplis and Geoff Marsh

Published by The Bardon Group Limited

The Bardon Group Limited
Unit 2 Cartwright Way
Forest Business Park
Coalville
LE67 1UE

First published 2014

ISBN 978-0-9928785-0-4

Designed and printed by Kall Kwik Bury St. Edmunds
www.kallkwikburystedmunds.co.uk

CONTENTS

PART ONE

In-Centre

"Keep in mind, this client has
very strong opinions."

> " Smile and greet customers as soon as they walk in – preferably by name and remember the customer is king! "

Make sure the Centre is clean and tidy at all times.

Don't allow your staff to eat, drink, smoke or shout – you're all on display!

The telephone should normally be answered within four rings. Treat every phone call as a potential customer placing an order. Take careful details of all customer information and the details of the job in question.

Ensure all staff know how to answer the telephone in a professional manner and are familiar with the message-taking procedure. For instance, if you need to collect customer data (name, postcode, mobile number, email etc) then put a procedure in place to incentivise/encourage staff to collect this data.

What your customer wants is a quality product and absolute dependability. Therefore take orders efficiently and professionally. **Don't promise deadlines you can't keep**, and keep all those promises you have undertaken.

Always ensure that customers are fully aware of what a job is likely to cost before proceeding and where possible collect money up front.

Ensure that branded promotional and customer-care items are used to promote the awareness of the brand within your market place.

Customer complaints should be resolved with speed and understanding to ensure customer satisfaction and lasting goodwill. Ensure all staff are trained in your complaint handling procedure.

Dress for success! Ensure your staff are always dressed in the corporate livery and that you the owner are professionally turned out.

PART TWO
CENTRE PRESENTATION

- Stand outside your Centre and take a critical look at the overall impact of the image you present to your customers. Does your Centre look like a business reflective of the services you offer?

- Ensure all exterior signs reflect current identity, are clean and properly lit. Replace worn out bulbs and tubes immediately.

- Keep windows clean and uncluttered. **Don't stick your own notices in the window, it will detract from the corporate identity and image.**

- Ensure that all staff are well presented and those facing customers are dressed smartly. Greet the customer upon entry in a pleasant professional manner.

- Keep customer areas free from deliveries and clutter e.g. put away supplies on arrival. It is essential that you keep the counter area clear for dealing with customers. It is at the counter that you can create a good impression and increase your order value.

- Ensure all work surfaces, floors, corridors and staircases are kept clean, tidy and free of deliveries, rubbish and dirt.

> Make sure all marketing materials and poster displays are fresh, simple and present a clear attractive sales message. Don't let them get stale, faded and dusty.

"Sorry for calling them 'graphics', Mr Burke. I meant the 'coloured pictures'."

PART THREE

PICTURE PERFECT

Getting a customer to come into your business is pretty fundamental to eventually doing any work for them. Customers can be timid creatures. If they sense any danger or discomfort they will run a mile. This begins when they are making the decision as to whether to open your door and enter or not.

Does it look clean?
Does it look bright?
Does it look safe?
Do I like the look of the people I can see inside?
Do I think I will feel comfortable in there?

When was the last time you stood outside your premises and looked in?

The famous filmmaker Walt Disney used to have a concept known as 'picture perfect' when he was creating his first theme park 'Disneyland' in California. Disney, being a filmmaker, would go round with a camera lens on a string around his neck.

He would randomly pick a spot in the Park and look through the lens at that spot and ask 'what's wrong with this picture?'. As a filmmaker he understood the importance of everything being 'picture perfect'. In a film everything has to look right. Anything that isn't will stick out like a sore thumb.

In the Disneyland Park Disney would look and see the lovely colourful fairytale characters, the fantasy castle, the fountains and the spectacular rides and then in the middle of the picture he would see dirty great dustbins. He recognised that all parks need dustbins but he immediately questioned as to whether they had to look so unattractive. And immediately Disney re-designed the bins to be more in-keeping with the rest of the Park.

"Sometimes it's good to get a different perspective."

The same principle should apply to your retail premises. Is it 'picture perfect'?

As a business owner it is your responsibility to do everything possible to make customers feel as welcome and safe as possible. It is not uncommon, over the years, for you and your staff to get used to dirty or untidy areas in the shop - the cracks in the walls or window areas, the water-damaged damp spots, the funny smells from the toilets or kitchen area. And, as many people do when they get used to something, they begin to forget about it or ignore it.

Customers, however, make no such allowances.

Have a fresh look. What is there in your premises that would put a customer off doing business with you?

PART FOUR
CENTRE OPERATIONS

- Ensure all staff are properly selected and trained in all the systems of the Centre. Refresh this training at regular intervals – procedures change and human beings forget and they cut-corners. Everyone needs a refresher on best practice now and again.

- Work in an organised, systematic manner and help your staff to do likewise. Follow the system – it works!

- Where problems arise, investigate the cause and take corrective action.

"A good team leader inspires intense loyalty."

- Welcome ideas and participation from staff and implement any genuine improvements suggested. Team spirit is essential.

- Ensure that clear definitions of responsibility exist within the Centre. Assign specific tasks to various people and check that they are performed with energy, accuracy and enthusiasm, however, don't allow demarcation lines to develop in your Centre. **All staff should be prepared to do whatever is needed, when needed.** This will mean that all staff need to know how to do everything in your Centre.

- Establish a regular starting up and closing procedure for you and your staff.

- Order consumables in good time making sure production is not disrupted through negligence.

- Carry out a daily 'work in progress' meeting with the staff to make sure the deadlines are met, and promises made to clients are kept!! Use these meetings to identify any shortcomings and discuss what can be done to overcome them. Everyone makes mistakes at some time. What is unacceptable is to keep making the same mistakes over and over again.

- One of the major challenges of the retail proposition is the static nature of the selling environment. Internet shopping is doing amazingly well because it has the capacity to go directly to the customer. For a premises based business you need the customer to come to you. However, premises based businesses are not precluded from hunting for business. As the owner of the business you need to incultate yourself into the local business community and it is your responsibility to interact with other retailers, service companies, agencies etc and encourage them to both give work to you and recommend you to others.

"This should make us more responsive."

PART FIVE

EMPLOYEE RELATIONS

"Everything on your CV is true...right?"

> **"** Hire quality people. Invest the time and effort it takes to recruit high performers. If you don't get it right the first time, cut your losses and try again. **"**

- Offer thorough and on-going training and development.

- Review performance of staff regularly, both informally and formally. Set clearly defined targets and objectives. Give constructive feedback and offer solutions.

- Treat staff in a professional, responsible and consistent manner and have on-going regular team and individual meetings to discuss progress, opportunities and duties.

- Showing appreciation for good work by rewarding quality, productivity, commitment and loyalty will go a long way to retaining good staff.

- All employees should have a contract of employment and job description and be aware of the terms and conditions of their employment.

- Treat staff fairly and encourage them to do likewise to each other and customers.

- Delegate tasks and develop the skills and responsibility levels of your staff.

- Create an atmosphere that is positive and effective. This will benefit you, your staff, your customers and ultimately your business.

A CEO of a large organisation was once asked how he managed to get such nice people in his organisation. He said 'It's easy – I hire nice people '

Getting your hiring procedure right is essential. NEVER TAKE SECOND BEST. If the person you want is not amongst your potential recruits then go and find some more recruits. If you have doubts before you take them on, you almost certainly will have those doubts confirmed once you have taken them on.

Once you have the right people you need to make sure they are delivering the very best service they can. Even the best of us need help in this area. You need to train your people and keep training them. We can always improve and always learn more. And once you have the right people you need to make sure you keep them.

PART SIX
SALES & MARKETING

Build relationships with your customers - be they domestic /residential, B2B or retail.

Only by getting close to your customers will you build up enough information to be able to offer valuable advice and increase order values. **Become their supplier of choice.**

Sales calls are an essential part of the system. It is your duty to apply the Sales Calling Programme diligently. So have a plan and follow it!

Use the necessary collateral and programmes available to you through your business systems.

Know your customers – keep your database up-to-date. Remember that as much as 20% of your database can be out of date after only 12 months. You need to keep up-to-date with customer emails, postcodes and mobile phone numbers.

PR (Public Relations) – Make use of local PR opportunities, and maintain regular contact with your PR agency. Coverage is never guaranteed but you could increase the chances of your Centre getting a mention by contacting the editors of your local media and building your own relationships. You could offer photographs of your Centre, arrange to be interviewed or give them case studies.

"Did you see a cocktail napkin with our entire marketing campaign on it?"

When marketing your Centre consider some or all of the following tools:

Leaflet drops
Press advertising
Advertorials
Networking
PR (yes worth mentioning twice!!)
E-Marketing
Social Media
Text Marketing
Involvement in the local community (sponsorships, charities, etc)
Local radio
Directories
Gimmicks?

The company's marketing strategy
became increasingly sophisticated.

Being a local business you will have benefited most by inculcating
yourself into the local community and becoming a 'face to be trusted'

PART SEVEN
QUALITY PRODUCT, QUALITY SERVICE

You can have spectacular premises, great marketing, and competitive pricing but if your service or products are not up to the mark you will not succeed as a business.

The high street is littered with the empty premises of businesses who had built no customer loyalty and a great deal of customer resentment, to the point that when the customers had an alternative they took it and the business was finished.

Microsoft was, for many years, the top brand in the world. Today it is behind both Apple and Google. Many customers used Microsoft despite being frustrated with software bugs, expensive products and never-ending software updates but when they finally could see an alternative way of satisfying their pc needs through Macs and Ipads, they took it.

"The client loves your work. Cut everything except for their logo."

You can be the biggest in the world but if you don't look after your customers you will not stay in business.

Adherence to your system is critical and ensuring everyone is trained in your system is vital.

PART EIGHT
COST EFFICIENT PRODUCTION

- Monitor cost of sales monthly

- Complete daily production schedules for all production staff. Compare expected production with actual results and with those of other Centres.

- Check supplier invoices received against purchase orders placed and delivery notes received. Ensure you receive all the discounts to which you are entitled and pay only for goods received.

- Ensure regular preventative maintenance is carried out on all machinery in accordance with the manufacturers' guidelines to prevent unnecessary downtown.

- Avoid discounting prices – this increases cost of sales and reduces margins. Offer your clients 'value for money' and 'added value' not cheap prices. Unless of course you are a commodity supplier in which case pricing may well be your key competitive edge.

- Organise and schedule all production work in accordance with the business system.

- Ensure overtime work is truly necessary and productive before authorising so that it does not become an easy perk for staff and a drain on your profitability!! Offer overtime only when a certain throughput has been achieved.

- Train and motivate staff to achieve maximum efficiency and encourage staff to offer ideas for improving systems when they see opportunities for doing so.

- Spot-check quality, wastage, material usage, cleanliness at random unannounced intervals. Complacency has no place in an active and successful business.

- Ensure all stock is correctly stored to avoid deterioration and unnecessary damage. Be careful not to over order.

"We succeeded in turning around the business ...
just in the wrong direction."

PART NINE

TECHNICAL MANAGEMENT

- Safety first – make sure equipment is properly guarded to British Safety Standards. Pay particular attention to electrical safety. Ensure all Health and Safety Standards are maintained.

- Keep any machinery in good working order by ensuring regular servicing, maintenance and cleaning. Keep a record of breakdowns and due service dates.

- Employ the best staff you can, someone who is going to be reliable, conscientious and productive. Ensure all staff receive adequate training in relation to their job descriptions.

- Keep a stock of all parts that need replacing and if in doubt speak to your supplier.

- Think before investing in additional equipment – 'Do I really need it? Can I really afford it? Will my clients and I profit from the investment?'

"I've done all my paper work. Need help with yours."

Employ the best staff you can, someone who is going to be reliable, conscientious and productive. Ensure all staff receive adequate training in relation to their job descriptions.

PART TEN
SUPPLIER RELATIONS

- Seek to develop good personal relations with all suppliers, treating them the way you like to be treated by your customers.

- Do not abuse the trading terms offered by your suppliers. Think also of your overall brand reputation in the industry.

- Don't allow personal friendliness to override business decisions in choosing a supplier, but once established on a proper business footing, do build on the relationship. You never know when you might need a favour!

- Always obtain regular and competitive quotes on all supply items to ensure you are not paying over the odds for products or services.

- Make maximum use of supplier promotional offers and discounts.

- Regularly update your supplier files and ensure you always have an alternative supplier on file as an emergency backup. Having a back-up supplier can also be very useful when it comes to negotiating with your suppliers. If your supplier thinks you have nowhere else to go you may find them less willing to give discounts or keep prices low.

- When ordering, always complete a purchase order, confirm when you will receive delivery of goods and record the details accordingly.

- Always check deliveries carefully, noting any discrepancies promptly. Ensure you check your supplier invoices carefully to ensure that you have only been charged for what you have actually received, at the price you are expecting.

- Keep copies of all correspondence with suppliers. If in dispute, write letters to confirm your position.

PART ELEVEN

Accounts & Book-Keeping

"What if we don't change at all ...
and something magical just happens?"

• Bring your accounts up-to-date at the end of every business day.

• Be aware of your financial position at the end of each day.

• Liquidity is essential for your survival.

• Complete your key performance indicators monthly and check reasons for discrepancies against targets.

• Regularly check your break-even analysis in relation to current cost of sales and whenever you experience changes in other costs.

• Always keep up to date with VAT and PAYE payments. In the same way keep your obligations with the bank.

• Take the maximum amount of credit offered by suppliers but do not amass large amounts of 'overdue' accounts.

- An annual Business Plan that contains budgets and sales projections is a must. A three-year Business Plan will motivate you to a greater profitability and success.

- Keep on top of your accounts or they will soon get on top of you! Most failed small businesses have neglected the book-keeping and financial management aspects of their business.

PART TWELVE
& THERE'S MORE...

Be persistent

Your own determination to succeed is essential to your eventual and continuing success.

Have Fun

Enjoy the process of building up a successful business. It will take a lot of hard work to achieve success. You might as well have fun doing it.

Maintain an open mind and flexibility of action.

Continue to learn and improve your understanding of your business and the industry.

"Hurry with the balloons!
We must get a more festive atmosphere!"

Delegate so that you can keep better employees, concentrate on the essentials and manage your time. To develop a successful business requires strategic thinking e.g 'where are we going to be in five years time and how are we going to get there?' If you don't delegate you will end up doing everything yourself and leave little or no time for the long-term development of your business.

Be structured and organised, consistent, ethical, planned, quality action is what counts.

Set your goals and then single-mindedly persist in reaching them. Your continuing unlimited dedication is your secret formula to success.

PART THIRTEEN

ABOUT THE AUTHORS

Nigel Toplis

Nigel Toplis is Managing Director of The Bardon Group – who specialise in developing and growing franchised businesses in the UK.

Nigel started his franchise career with Kall Kwik the specialist high street print and design franchise and was Managing Director until he left in December 2002 to join Recognition Express.

As with Kall Kwik, Recognition Express started its life in 1979 and like Kall Kwik it is solely a B2B franchise – specialising in personalised name badges, signs, clothing and promotional gifts.

In addition to Recognition Express, Nigel franchises ComputerXplorers, which provides ICT education to 3-13 year olds, under a master franchise arrangement from the American owner and in January 2011 formally launched a third franchise – The ZipYard – a high street operation specialising in garment alterations.

In January 2012 Nigel took on the master licence for Kall Kwik thus returning to his franchise roots.

Nigel has written two books on franchising, was previously Chairman of the bfa and is a Fellow of Lancaster University.

Geoff Marsh

A graduate of the University of Loughborough, Geoff started his career as an actor before becoming a presenter in 1986 on the Lloyds Bank's 'Customer First' Programme. This was one of the largest series of roadshow workshops in the world and was seen by approximately 70,000 staff.

As a trainer and presenter, Geoff has been involved with conferences, seminars and training programmes for organisations such as Wessex Water, Sun Microsystems,

Scottish & Newcastle Breweries, Forte Hotels and Kall Kwik.

Geoff is an international trainer and presenter and frequently works outside the UK for organisations such as Lloyds Bank International Private Banking, BNP Paribas, HSBC, Union Bancaire Privee and Unichem.

He is a visiting lecturer on the Swiss Banking School's prestigious executive MBA programme. He has also worked with the Financial Times on their Wealth Management Academy Series.

In addition Geoff is also much sought after as a presenter and after-dinner speaker. He has his own weekly radio show with Swindon FM.

This year he has also launched his first Training Video with Temple Video Productions – Powerful Presentations.

He has been a professional actor on stage, television and even cruise ships.

"With our pioneering spirit we are
going to break into some great new markets."